SEVEN
POWER PRINCIPLES

THAT I DIDN'T LEARN
IN SEMINARY

SEVEN
POWER PRINCIPLES

THAT I DIDN'T LEARN
IN SEMINARY

C. PETER WAGNER

Wagner Publications

Seven Power Principles That I Didn't Learn in Seminary
Copyright © 2000
by C. Peter Wagner
ISBN 1-58502-014-1

Published by
Wagner Publications
11005 N. Highway 83
Colorado Springs, CO 80921
www.wagnerpublications.org

Cover design by
Erin Mathis
emdesign Studio
63 Poinsettia Avenue
San Mateo, CA 94403
www.emdesignstudio.com

Interior design by
Rebecca Sytsema

Rights for publishing this book in other languages are contracted by Gospel Literature International (GLINT). GLINT also provides technical help for the adaptation, translation, and publishing of Bible study resources and books in scores of languages worldwide. For further information, contact GLINT, P.O. Box 4060, Ontario, CA 91761-1003, USA. You may also send e-mail to glintint@aol.com, or visit their web site at www.glint.org.

1 2 3 4 5 6 7 8 9   06 05 04 03 02 01 00

CONTENTS

SOME KNOWN LIMITATIONS OF SEMINARY TRAINING

For two or three generations there has been an assumption here in America that clergy need to be educated on at least the undergraduate, and preferably the graduate level in order to command respect in their communities and to serve their congregations as they should. Many traditional denominations still will not consider ordaining an individual unless they first earn a Bible college or a seminary degree.

I must say that for generations the system worked fairly well. American churches, by and large, have flourished and for much of American history, they constituted a vital sector of American society in general. This, however, is much less the case today than it was previously. The change began to come toward the end of the 1960s when what were considered the mainline denominations began to decline—a decline which continues today. Even the Southern Baptists, which for years were the rare exception, actually declined in membership in 1998, the first time that had happened since 1926.

New Wineskins
Replacing Old Ones

What is going on? Study the growth of churches in almost any metropolitan area of the country and you will find a number of churches which are growing vigorously, some of them megachurches of several thousand members. By and large, these churches function very differently from the traditional churches in the city. Many of them do not belong to any of the mainline denominations, and even those which do, have, for the most part, long since been coloring outside of their standard denominational lines.

These churches comprise what could be seen as a new wineskin for American Christianity. Other parts of the world are experiencing similar phenomena. I call this the "New Apostolic Reformation," and I have written several books analyzing the extraordinary growth dynamics of these churches. It is not my desire to rehash that information in this book, but I do want to move into an area that is not found in my other books, namely the supernatural power that is characteristic of most of the churches of the New Apostolic Reformation. I chose the title, *Seven Power Principles That I Didn't Learn in Seminary,* because so many clergy who are seminary graduates will be able to identify with where I have come from and with what I am saying.

Seminaries Do Teach Power

Four decades ago, I took my training for ministry in what were then and still are considered excellent seminaries, Fuller Theological Seminary and Princeton Theological Seminary. I am truly thankful for the theological education that I received at both places, and I know that I would not be where I am now without what they provided. But as I now look at those seminaries and scores of others like them from the perspective of the 21st century, it is clear to me that they were designed to serve what are now the old wineskins, namely the denominations. The seminaries I chose were typical. Princeton was owned and operated by a traditional denomination, namely the Presbyterian Church. Fuller was independent, but its mission statement declared that it was founded in order to serve

---

*I was taught nothing
about God's power for miracles
in the church and in the world today!*

---

the mainline denominations.

As I studied in these seminaries, did I learn about the power of God? Yes, I certainly did. I learned that one of the attributes of God was omnipotence, meaning that He was all-powerful and that there was nothing He was incapable of doing. I learned that He had power to save the lost and to transform us into new creatures in Christ Jesus. I learned that He gives us power to overcome sin and to live holy lives. I learned that He was King of kings and Lord of lords.

But, having said this, I was taught nothing about God's power for miracles in the church and in the world today!

Why?

Warfield's Cessationism

In both of the seminaries I attended, my professors believed what is called cessationist theology. The theologian to whom they referred the most was Benjamin Breckenridge Warfield, a professor at Princeton Seminary in the early part of the century. Warfield was able to persuade a whole generation of Christian leaders that the supernatural works of God that we read about in the New Testament were necessary only in the beginning stages of the church. After the apostolic age, particularly when the canon of Scripture was finally agreed upon, the miraculous acts characteristic of the apostles had ceased, thus the label "cessationism."

Elmer Towns says it as well as anyone, "The typical systematic theology textbook in use in evangelical Bible colleges and theological seminaries in North America includes a passing reference to the reality of supernatural spiritual beings. The diligent theology student learns the devil is an angel who went bad, demons are the third of the angels who rebelled with him and the angels are the good guys that stayed good. A belief in spiritual beings remains a part of our orthodox view of theology, but there appears to be little interest on the part of theologians to apply this doctrine in any practical way."[1]

A Radical Paradigm Shift

This was my way of thinking through about my first twenty years of ministry. But then I went through a radical paradigm shift. Here are several things that I now believe:

♦ *Understanding the modus operandi of angels and demons is a high priority for effective ministry.* I never denied that angels and demons existed, but for years I had no idea of how they operated in everyday life.

♦ *Power ministries are vital for maximizing gospel outreach.*

They include healings, miracles, prophecy, tongues, deliverance, spiritual warfare, and other ministry activities.

◆ *Sources of information about the invisible world are not
limited to the Bible.* Arriving at this conclusion was a
major revision of what I was taught about epistemology
in seminary. I firmly continue to believe that the Bible is
our principal and only inerrant source of information about
the supernatural. What the Bible teaches cannot be con-
tradicted. But the Bible is not our only source. For one
thing, while God spoke through the Bible, He also speaks
today and He frequently gives us new information. Even
the dark side of the invisible world can provide us some
valuable information as well if we are careful to filter it
through lenses of sanctified discernment.

What I have just described is the paradigm of most new apostolic leaders today. This is part and parcel of the new wineskin
that God is shaping for the church of the future. In 1996 I
convened what was called the National Symposium on the
Postdenominational Church. In it more than 40 leaders of the
New Apostolic Reformation took the platform to express the
way they are seeing the moves of God in the church today. I
will not soon forget the way that Pastor Gary Greenwald of
Eagle's Nest in Irvine, California dealt with the issue of supernatural phenomena in apostolic churches at that symposium.

Supernatural Phenomena

Gary Greenwald said, "Most of you are here today because
you are curious about the spiritual phenomena that are happening all around the world today. Our panel will be talking

about things like drunkenness and laughing, people falling and shaking violently, outbreaks of miraculous healings, prophetic conventions where teams of men and women deliver personal prophecies to many, outrageous meetings where demons are manifesting and people are being set free, strange acts like strong winds suddenly blowing through congregations, blowing everyone's hair back, blowing individuals off piano benches, drops of oil falling inside buildings, everybody's Bible getting covered with drops of oil, people frozen in one position for hours, unable to move, and all kinds of other manifestations and phenomena."[2]

I fully realize that Greenwald's description of religious experience is uncomfortable to many of today's Christian leaders who hold degrees from Bible colleges or from seminaries. In fact I can well imagine that some would have relegated such behavior to the lunatic fringe. Nevertheless, the fastest growing segment of Christianity, not only in America, but even more in other parts of the world, is not only comfortable with such supernatural manifestations in their churches, but they fully expect God to work that way on a fairly regular basis.

Let me be clear that not every church which I would associate with the New Apostolic Reformation would operate within a philosophy of ministry which embraces all the apostolic power principles which I am going to describe in this book. As I explain in detail in some of my other books, the New Apostolic Reformation includes both charismatic and non-charismatic churches.

I do not have hard facts, but my guess is that, in America, perhaps 20 percent of the apostolic churches would be traditional evangelical churches. Few would be cessationists, but they would typically choose not to feature the kind of outward, supernatural phenomena that Gary Greenwald describes in their day-to-day and week-to-week church activities. Many of them are growing vigorously without such manifestations.

God's Power in the World

However, outside of North America, particularly in Third World nations, the percentage of new apostolic churches which would not practice these power principles outwardly would be extremely small. For example, Mike Berg and Paul Pretiz spent years researching the fastest growing churches of Latin America, which turned out to be what they call "grass roots churches," and what I call "new apostolic churches." Almost all of them were pastored by leaders who had never been influenced by foreign missionaries and who had not attended mission-founded Bible schools or seminaries.

As part of their research, Berg and Pretiz contrasted these grass roots churches to the mission-related churches in Latin America which tended to be more traditionally evangelical in nature, and which, generally speaking, were not growing like the others. Here is one of their significant conclusions, "The real issue is whether mission-related churches can understand and adopt the best of a pre-Enlightenment worldview that is common to the masses in Latin America. This is a view that is open to the miraculous, to God's intervention in daily experience, to biblical confrontation with the demonic, and to a focus in worship that emphasizes reveling in God's presence rather than passive participation in a cerebrally oriented service."[3]

Looking Ahead

With this as a background, let's now take a look at seven of the apostolic power principles commonly accepted and practiced in new apostolic churches. I had to learn all of them after graduating from seminary!

Notes

1. Elmer L. Towns and Neil T. Anderson, *Rivers of Revival* (Ventura CA: Regal Books, 1997), p.219.
2. Gary Greenwald, statement transcribed from an audio tape in the National Symposium on the Postdenominational Church held in Pasadena, California, May 22, 1996.
3. Clayton L. ["Mike"] Berg and Paul E. Pretiz, "Latin America's Fifth Wave of Protestant Churches," *International Bulletin of Missionary Research,* October 1996, p. 159.

THE OPERATIONAL ROLE
OF THE HOLY SPIRIT

In new apostolic churches, day in and day out, references to the person and work of the Holy Spirit are much more frequent than in traditional churches.

Why would this be the case?

I think that we have two underlying reasons why it is true. These reasons are closely connected with each other.

Focusing on the Future

The first factor has to do with focus. New apostolic churches are essentially driven by vision. There is a mindset characteristic of leaders of apostolic churches which differs considerably from the mindset we have become used to in traditional Christianity. As we know, the traditional organizational structure for bringing churches together has been denominations. Denominational leaders tend to focus on the present and then draw from the past. Most denominations were founded by strong, visionary leaders. While they rarely used the term, they were, almost without exception, apostles. The first generation of the denomination frequently turned out to be the most glorious generation in the denomination's history.

Following the normal sociological pattern of organizational life cycles, most denominations began to routinize after the first generation. Administrators generally replaced the visionary, apostolic founders. Godly as these administrators might have been, they would typically see their role as perpetuating the vision of the founder, not casting new vision for the denomination themselves. That is why I said that they tend to focus on the present and draw from the past. When things slow down, they will frequently say, "We need to get back to our roots!"

New apostolic church leaders have quite a different focus. They begin with the future and draw from the present. Their vision for the future is a God-ordained reality, not simply a desired possibility. They will, therefore, adjust the present in any way possible so that the vision will be fulfilled. This introduces a dimension of consecrated pragmatism into the mindset of apostolic leaders that their more traditional counterparts often criticize. Apostolic leaders will characteristically say, "We know where God wants us to go, and we'll do whatever it takes to get there!"

Reaching the Lost

That leads me to the second factor contributing to the high profile emphasis on the Holy Spirit in apostolic churches. It is the driving desire to reach out to the lost, which is part of the DNA of apostolic churches. What does it take to reach the lost? It takes the power of the Holy Spirit. This is not simply a theologically correct statement. It is a driving operational force. It comes from the premise that the Holy Spirit is the person of the Trinity most directly involved in effective evangelism. Saying this does not reduce the emphasis on the Father and the Son in apostolic churches, but it clearly does increase the emphasis on the Holy Spirit.

This is not only a pragmatic conclusion based on the premise that the more we have the Holy Spirit the more we'll evangelize. It is all of that, but it is also understood as a biblical principle. While I was in seminary, I was taught that an indispensable lens through which I should interpret the Bible was "the cross." Before coming to a conclusion on any doctrine or important idea for ministry, I was taught to ask the test question: How does this relate to "the cross?" Behind this was an assumption that our focus should constantly be on the work of the Second Person of the Trinity.

"Cross" or "Charisma?"

Since graduating from seminary, however, I have met an increasing number of effective Christian leaders who do not question in the slightest that the work of Jesus on the cross is foundational to all that we believe and do, but who, at the same time, would not regard the cross as the major compass point for moving ahead in active ministry. A much more determinative compass point for them would generally be "charisma," focusing on the work of the Third Person of the Trinity rather than on the Second Person of the Trinity.

As I have meditated on this interesting contrast between "cross" and "charisma," it has become clear to me that Jesus Himself would have taught His apostles to choose "charisma," or the work of the Holy Spirit, as their guidance for the way to do ministry such as evangelism. No one taught me that in seminary.

Let me explain.

Recognizing Who Jesus Is

By the time of the events recorded in Matthew 16, Jesus' disciples had been with Him for a year and a half. Jesus asked them who the people out there were saying He was. The disciples reported that some thought He was John the Baptist and some thought He was Elijah or Jeremiah or one of the prophets. Jesus was obviously setting them up for the next question: "Who do *you* say that I am?" Peter, speaking for the group, responded, "You are the Christ, the Son of the Living God" (Matt. 16:16).

This is an extremely important statement, because it is the first time, after a year and a half, that the disciples were able to verbalize accurately that they recognized Jesus as the Messiah ("Christ" being the Greek for the Hebrew "Messiah") for whom the Jews had been waiting for centuries.

Why Jesus Came

Jesus then immediately replied, "On this rock I will build My church" (Matt. 16:18). This is the first time that Jesus ever mentioned the church to His disciples. Why? Jesus, very simply, could not tell his disciples why he had come until they first were very sure that they knew who He was.

Then He told them that building the church would entail spiritual warfare, because He said, "The gates of Hades shall not prevail against it" (Matt. 16:18). Obviously, Satan and his gates of Hades would try their best to stop the growth of the church, but they would not succeed because Jesus would give His disciples the keys of the kingdom. These keys would obviously open the opposing gates so that the kingdom of God could advance across the earth. The keys that the disciples had would be "binding" and "loosing," terms directly related to spiritual warfare.

The Shock: Jesus Was Leaving!

The disciples obviously received all of this, and they were saying to themselves that they would be more than ready to move forward with Jesus, in order to expand the kingdom of God throughout the earth. What they were not ready for, however, was Jesus' next statement that He would soon die and that He would not be with them any more. In other words, for the future extension of the kingdom, Jesus' apostles would be on their own!

This was too much for Peter. He protested and argued with Jesus so strongly that Jesus had to rebuke him by saying, "Get behind Me, Satan!" (Matt. 16:23). It must have been quite a scene!

When things calmed down, Jesus then explained to His disciples that, amazingly enough, it would actually be to their *advantage* if He left them. How could that be? How could anything be better than having Jesus present with them in person as they went forth to minister?

The Advantage of the Holy Spirit

Here is how Jesus explained it to them: "I tell you the truth. It is to your advantage that I go away; for if I do not go away, the Helper will not come to you; but if I depart, I will send Him to you" (John 16:7). The "Helper," of course, is the Holy Spirit. What Jesus was telling His disciples, then, is the point I am trying to make in this chapter, namely that *for the purpose of evangelism, the immediate presence of the Third Person of the Trinity is more important than the immediate presence of the Second person of the Trinity!*

This is what I never learned in Seminary. It is why some dynamic leaders of churches today choose the paradigm of "charisma" rather than the paradigm of the "cross" to guide their ministry. They are choosing the Third Person of the Trinity, just as Jesus instructed His disciples to do.

Jesus did spend another year and a half with His disciples. They received excellent training for ministry, not in a class-room working toward a degree, but out in the field learning by apprenticeship. By the time they finished, they had learned preaching, evangelism, morals, ethics, theology, Old Testament, prophecy, healing, deliverance, prayer, spiritual warfare, and many other things. They had received a commission to

> *No amount of learning*
> *can substitute for ministry*
> *done by the operational power*
> *of the Holy Spirit.*

go into all the world and to preach the gospel to every crea-ture. No other group of people has ever been better prepared to aggressively spread the message of the kingdom of God.

However, Jesus made sure that His disciples knew that all this good training would not be enough. After His resurrec-tion and while He was still with His disciples, He told them that after He left they should not immediately go out and start preaching the gospel. If they did, all their training would be for nothing. No, first they should "tarry in the city of Jerusalem until you are endued with power from on high" (Luke 24:49).

Just as He was ready to leave, Jesus reminded them of this. His very last words on earth were: "You shall receive power when the Holy Spirit has come upon you; and you shall be witnesses to Me in Jerusalem, and in all Judea and Samaria, and to the end of the earth" (Acts 1:8). Fortunately, the disciples did what they were told, and on the day of Pentecost they were filled with the Holy Spirit.

The "Operational" Role of the Holy Spirit

This is what I mean by the term, the "operational" role of the Holy Spirit. I was, of course, taught about the Holy Spirit in seminary. I was taught that He was omnipotent, omniscient, and omnipresent. I was taught to sing, "Praise Him above ye heavenly host, praise Father, Son and Holy Ghost!" I took a subject called "pneumatology," which is the doctrine of the Holy Spirit. But I was never taught how to tarry until I was endued with the filling and the power of the Holy Spirit as were Jesus' apostles in the first century. In other words, I knew the *theology* of the Holy Spirit, but I was virtually ignorant of the present day *operation* of the Holy Spirit.

Apostolic churches are not embarrassed by frequent references to the immediate operation of the Holy Spirit in their sermons, in their songs, in their prayers, and in general conversation among believers. They teach on the baptism of the Holy Spirit and the ministry of the Holy Spirit. They frequently speak directly to the Holy Spirit and pray words to the effect, "Holy Spirit, we invite you to come and minister to us right now!"

I see this as a very significant power principle, which has both biblical and practical justification. It is a major reason why apostolic churches today are winning more lost people to Jesus Christ than other churches. It is simply a matter of understanding and applying what Jesus meant when He said that the presence of the Holy Spirit is an advantage to those who desire to spread the gospel.

No amount of learning can substitute for ministry done by the operational power of the Holy Spirit.

PRINCIPLE TWO:

WARFARE
WORSHIP

In her book *Possessing the Gates of the Enemy,* Cindy Jacobs tells a revealing story. She was in a women's meeting in which a member of the audience came to the front with tears streaming down her face. She was suffering with a serious problem of depression for which she had to be hospitalized on occasion. Even at the moment, she appeared to be on the verge of a nervous breakdown. Several others gathered around and they started to pray, although with no visible results. The symptoms continued. Then someone called for a worship leader to come forward.

Cindy says, "I went to the piano, and we began a type of warfare that is becoming quite frequent in prayer groups today—warring against the works of Satan by worshipping the Lord . . .

"The women in the seminar stood to their feet. They sang; they clapped; they shouted; until suddenly the woman for whom they were praying began to weep and relate that the oppression had completely left her mind. It was as though a cloud had lifted, and for the first time in years her thoughts were clear. How we rejoiced together at the goodness of God on her behalf!"[1]

One-Hour Worship Services

I took a course in seminary on worship and worship services. I was taught that the worship service lasts about one hour, and, while there is room for some variation, it usually contains three congregational hymns, one choir anthem, an invocation, a pastoral prayer, a benediction, announcements, the offering, a Scripture reading, and a sermon. The congregation would usually stand for the invocation, the first hymn, the hymn just before the sermon, and the benediction.

Things are quite different now. The church I belong to, New Life Church of Colorado Springs, features services that are two hours long. Worship usually occupies the first 45 minutes or so, with the congregation on its feet all that time. When worship is over, announcements and greetings take some 15 minutes, and then we move from worship to "the word" followed by an altar call for the last hour.

Dynamic Participation in Worship

The first thing that impresses a visitor to a new apostolic church like New Life is that singing songs of worship and praise takes almost as much time as the entire traditional "worship service" used to take. The second thing is that the audience seems to be drawn more deeply into dynamic participation in the worship, versus routine performance in traditional services.

In traditional churches, the congregational hymns are seen as useful for preparing the congregation for the central focus of the service, namely the sermon. In new apostolic churches, however, it is different. True, the sermon is usually longer than in traditional churches. But new apostolic worship is not so much preparation for the sermon as it is a powerful spiritual experience on its own merits. Church attendees expect the power of God to move on them as much or even more in the worship time than in listening to the word. Singing worship songs often connects them in heart and soul more directly with God than does learning about the Bible and the Christian life during the sermon time.

Worship, interspersed, as it invariably is, with times of prayer, becomes the expected opening for the power of God to come upon the people who attend church. The quality of

---

The major effect of worship is often not on the worshipers themselves, but it can and does also produce a strong influence in the invisible world.

---

worship therefore sets the tone for the whole service. In reality the people are more spiritually prepared for the sermon than in many traditional churches. This is why I include worship as one of the seven power principles in this book.

Warfare Worship

But I want to take it even one step further. The major effect of worship is often not on the worshipers themselves, but it can and does also produce a strong influence in the invisible world.

When God is glorified, His power and His light increase proportionately. Simultaneously, the forces of darkness in the invisible world can be pushed back and weakened so that they will have less probability of obstructing the purposes of God here on earth. It is at this point that worship can become a powerful weapon of spiritual warfare. This is what gives currency to the term that I have used in the title of this chapter, "warfare worship."

Let's take a look at some biblical examples of warfare worship.

The Church in Jerusalem

When the church was first founded in Jerusalem, it engaged in warfare worship. The believers continued daily in the temple and they were seen as "*praising God* and having favor with all the people" (Acts 2:47, italics added). This resulted in effective evangelism because "the Lord added to the church daily those who were being saved" (Acts 2:47). Actually, the disciples had been in the temple ever since Jesus had left them: "And they were continually in the temple praising and blessing God" (Luke 24:53). The purpose of being in the temple was to worship God.

This temple in Jerusalem was the same temple that Jesus had cleansed a while before by driving out the moneychangers. My point is that when Jesus cleansed the temple, He quoted two Old Testament Scriptures, both relevant to warfare worship (see Matt. 21:12-16):

♦ *Isaiah 56:7*: "My house shall be called a house of prayer." The word "prayer" here is the Hebrew *tephillah,* which means "psalm" or prayer set to music. It is another word for what we call "worship."

♦ *Psalm 8:2:* "Out of the mouths of babes and infants You have perfected praise." The children in the temple who were saying, "Hosanna to the Son of David!" triggered this quote from Jesus. But Psalm 8, not Matthew 21, gives us the specific purpose of this "perfected praise." It was to "silence the enemy and the avenger!" Warfare worship will do this. It will prevent Satan and his forces in the demonic world from accomplishing their evil purposes!

This early group of believers who were doing warfare worship in the temple were biblical believers. However their only Bible was the Old Testament. It is a safe assumption, therefore, that they were being guided in doing this by Old Testament teachings. I suppose that they would have been familiar with such passages as these:

♦ *Psalm 22:3:* "But You are holy, who inhabit the praises of Israel." God inhabits or dwells personally in the praises of His people. The word "praises" is again *tephillah*, which we understand as worship. This tells us that during worship, the immediate presence of God is expected to be stronger than when we do not worship. The early believers would have known this.

♦ *Psalm 149:5-9:* "Let the saints be joyful in glory; let them sing aloud on their beds. Let the high praises of God be in their mouth, and a two-edged sword in their hand to execute vengeance on the nations, and punishments on the peoples, *to bind their kings with chains and their nobles with fetters of iron*; to execute on them the written judgment." I italicized "binding kings and nobles" because the phrase is an Old Testament equivalent of "binding the strongman" in the New Testament (see Matt. 12:29). This would have given the early believers courage to know that their warfare worship in the temple could actually neutralize the power of the enemy.

♦ *2 Chronicles 20.* The believers in the temple had heard the story of Jehoshaphat, the king of Judah, when he came up against the powerful armies of Moab, Ammon, and Mount Seir. Jehoshaphat was frightened (20:3). He thought he did not have enough power to withstand them (20:12). He had no idea what to do (20:12). But then the prophet spoke and said to Jehoshaphat, "The battle is not yours, but God's" (20:15), and the king then decided that his best strategy would be warfare worship. So "He appointed those who should sing to the Lord, and who should praise the beauty of holiness" (20:21). The next thing he knew, his enemies had all killed each other and "there were their dead bodies, fallen on the earth. None had escaped!" (20:24). Jehoshaphat discovered that warfare worship really works!

♦ *2 Kings 3.* The kings of Israel, Judah and Edom were in trouble. They set out to fight the king of Moab, but all their armies with all their animals became marooned in the desert without water. They asked Elisha the prophet to help them. What did Elisha do? He commanded warfare worship by saying, "bring me a musician." The result? "When the musician played, the hand of the Lord came upon him" (3:15). God sent water supernaturally, and the king of Moab was defeated. The armies that won the battle won because of warfare worship!

Paul and Silas' Escape

The gospel had begun to spread from Jerusalem into Europe. Paul was in Philippi with his apostolic team. He cast a demon out and the resulting uproar was so bad that Paul and Silas found themselves severely beaten and thrown into the inner prison with their feet in stocks. There seemed to be no hope. Their skin was torn and bleeding, the floor was hard and filthy, they were stripped and the prison was cold, they were exhausted, and they were totally immobile. By midnight the average prisoners would have moaned and groaned and dozed into a fitful sleep.

But not Paul and Silas. "At midnight Paul and Silas were praying and singing hymns to God" (Acts 16:25). This was warfare worship at its best. An earthquake came, all the prisoners were freed, and the jailer later received Jesus Christ as his Lord and Savior. Worship opened the way for God to accomplish His plan here on earth.

Testing the Missionary

Sometimes I wonder what would have happened if I had been taught warfare worship in seminary before I became a missionary to Bolivia. I might have seen things happen like Sam Sasser did. Sam Sasser, a missionary to the South Pacific, told me that he was the first missionary to visit one of the tropical islands there. He approached the chief and asked permission to preach the gospel to his people. The chief said, "Yes, but first you must pass some tests." Sam agreed.

Twelve strong young men came out and challenged Sam

to match them in certain feats of prowess, which Sam readily did. Then the chief said, "You have done well. There is one more test." At that point the twelve men started a dance to the beat of drums, designed to call down the territorial spirit whom Satan had assigned to the island. When they had reached a certain frenzy, three young women entered the middle of the circle and they also started to dance. In a short time the three began rising and suddenly they were dancing in the air about ten feet off the ground!

Can Your God Do That?

The chief, with a wry look in his eye, turned to Sam Sasser and said, "Missionary, can your God do that?" After a pause, Sam said to the chief, "Sir, my God is not in the levitating business. But I'll tell you what He *can* do. He can make those girls come back down!"

With that, Sam Sasser turned his back on the occult display. He didn't have a piano to play as Cindy Jacobs did. Nevertheless, he took a couple of steps, raised both arms toward heaven and began to sing loud praises to God. It wasn't long before the three girls came crashing to the ground! One of them even sprained her ankle in the process and she was seen limping around the village for a few days afterward.

Sam Sasser understood warfare worship!

The chief turned to Sam and said, "Missionary, you now have my permission to preach the gospel to my people!"

Notes

1. Cindy Jacobs, *Possessing the Gates of the Enemy* (Grand Rapids MI: Chosen Books, 1994), pp. 172-173.

PRINCIPLE THREE:

PROPHECY:
HEARING THE VOICE OF GOD

I was recently handed a list of the ten greatest revivals in history and asked to choose the revival that has most affected me personally. Without hesitation I chose the Pentecostal revival which occurred at the beginning of the 20th century.

How would something that happened so long ago affect me? I wasn't even alive at the time. To my knowledge, none of my ancestors were Pentecostal. The church I joined when I was saved in 1950 was *anti*-Pentecostal. I served as a missionary under two mission boards which would go so far as to dismiss missionaries if they were caught speaking in tongues.

A Radical Paradigm Shift

At this point I am not going to describe the details of the

radical, although gradual, paradigm shift which I experienced beginning around 1970. But as I came to understand and experience the power of the Third Person of the Trinity, who began to come into His rightful place with the Pentecostal revival about one hundred years ago, my entire ministry soared to a new level which I could not have imagined previously.

Because this paradigm shift was so radical, I carefully observed and analyzed its various steps and phases. There were many new things I had to get used to. Some were easier than others. As I look back, however, it is clear that the most radical of the mental, spiritual, and intellectual challenges that I faced related to the topic of this chapter. Let me highlight this by setting it in bold type:

God speaks directly to His people today!

Some would be surprised to find how many intelligent, good-hearted Christians cannot come to believe this. They think that all of God's revelation to His people is in the Bible. This, for example, is what one of the most famous and respected Christian leaders in America today, John MacArthur, sincerely believes. MacArthur wrote a book, *Charismatic Chaos,* in 1992 in which he attempts to disprove many of the major distinctives of Pentecostals and charismatics. It is very significant that the title of his first chapter is: "Does God Still Give Revelation?"

MacArthur's answer to that question is the same one I would have given before my paradigm shift. His general thesis is: No! God does not still give revelation. Here are his exact words: "Scripture is a closed system of truth, complete, sufficient, and not to be added to (Jude 3; Rev.

22:18-19). It contains all the spiritual truth God intended to reveal."[1]

Reformed Theology

This is good Reformed theology. It is the standard belief of the churches which have come down to us from John Calvin, John Knox, and Abraham Kuyper. The two seminaries I went to, Fuller and Princeton, both identified themselves as Reformed seminaries. While I was in Princeton, I was taught that the doctrinal paradigm of the Presbyterian Church is molded by the Westminster Confession of Faith, which says:

> "The whole counsel of God, concerning all things necessary for his own glory, man's salvation, faith, and life is either expressly set down in Scripture, or by good and necessary consequence may be deduced from Scripture: unto which nothing at any time is to be added, whether by new revelations of the Spirit or traditions of men" (1:6).

Needless to say, prophecy was not a power principle that I was taught in seminary.

Jack Deere's Paradigm Shift

Jack Deere, arguably, has helped more people move from a cessationist paradigm to a power paradigm than anyone else because of the influence of his two major books: *Surprised by the Power of the Spirit* (Zondervan) and *Surprised by the Voice of God* (Zondervan). He was actually dismissed from the faculty of Dallas Theological Seminary because he adopted the power paradigm, so he has paid a considerable personal price for the change.

When he started to write *Surprised by the Power of the Spirit* Deere was going to include a chapter on prophecy. But the more he studied it, the more he realized that the issues raised with prophecy merited, not a chapter, but a whole new book. Here is what he says in *Surprised by the Power of the Spirit*: "The most difficult transition for me in my pilgrimage was not in accepting that Scripture teaches that God heals and does miracles today through gifted believers. The thing I resisted the most, was most afraid of, and which took the most convincing was accepting that God still *speaks* today."[2]

The New Wineskin

As I have said many times, God has provided a new wineskin for His cutting-edge church of the 21st century. With few exceptions, the leaders of the churches of the New Apostolic Reformation are no longer questioning whether God speaks to His people today. As I analyze the big picture, three characteristics of new apostolic leaders which relate to prophecy stand out in my mind:

1. New Apostolic Reformation churches accept the spiritual gift of prophecy.

Most all of the new apostolic leaders I know give a literal interpretation to the Bible verses which tell us that God gives gifts of prophecy to certain members of the body of Christ. Romans 12 and 1 Corinthians 12 are the two most detailed biblical passages on spiritual gifts. Here is what they say:

Romans 12:6: Having then gifts differing according to

the grace that is given to us, let us use them: if prophecy, let us prophesy in proportion to our faith.

1 Corinthians 12: (1) Now concerning spiritual gifts, brethren, I do not want you to be ignorant . . . (7) But the manifestation of the Spirit is given to each one for the profit of all . . . (10) to another the working of miracles, to another prophecy. . .

The Gift of Prophecy

I believe that every Christian has the ability to hear the voice of God. As my paradigm shift progressed, I began to develop the ability to hear what the Holy Spirit was saying directly. Previously I am sure that the Holy Spirit was leading me in ways other than speaking directly to me, such as through bringing certain circumstances into my life. But now I am convinced that I was, at that time, operating under God's "Plan B." God's "Plan A" is for each believer to be in such intimate relation-

---

God's "Plan A" is for each believer to be in such intimate relationship to Him through the filling of the Holy Spirit that He can literally communicate what is in His heart with us.

---

ship to Him through the filling of the Holy Spirit that He can literally communicate what is in His heart with us.

When I was in seminary, no one taught me that prayer was ordinarily two-way prayer. None of my professors ever said, "When I was praying this morning, God spoke to me and said so-and-so." The general idea was that we pray by talking to God, and then we wait until we see some visible evidence that God, in His sovereignty, has decided to answer our prayer. I will admit that this procedure does kick in from time to time, but that is not all there is to prayer. Prayer should ideally be a two-way conversation between us and God. We speak to our Heavenly Father and He speaks back to us, just as our earthly father would do if we were having a telephone conversation with Him.

In my experience the most challenging thing, once I believed that I could actually hear from God, was to be able to tell the difference between God's voice and my own thoughts. Since God doesn't often speak in an audible voice, this is something that each one of has to learn how to do. I say "learn" because the more you concentrate on making it happen, the more it will happen. And the learning is also a process. At the beginning you might not be very good at it, but over time your ability to distinguish what God is saying becomes more accurate.

I have now come to the point where, from time to time, God has spoken to me so clearly that I can virtually say, "I quote." Granted the "quotes" are usually my best paraphrases, but for the most part they are pretty accurate. And, given my current position of leadership, some of these revelations from God are not relatively minor things such as where I should go on vacation or if I should buy a new car, but they influence fairly significant segments of the whole body of Christ. Do I ever make mistakes? Sure I do, but that's part of the risk of stepping out in faith. To minimize the risk, I have a close circle of colleagues with whom I test these words from the Lord, especially if they would affect other people. In doing this, I hopefully discover the wrong ones before it is too late.

Do I Have the Gift?

One of the reasons that I gave so much detail about my own experience of learning how to hear from God was for me to go on from there and point this out: *I do not have the spiritual gift of prophecy*!

Those who have read my book *Your Spiritual Gifts Can Help Your Church Grow* (Regal Books) will understand the important difference between "Christian roles" and "spiritual gifts." Just like every Christian has a *role* of being an effective witness for Christ, not everyone has the *gift* of evangelist, the same goes with prophecy. Every Christian has a *role* of hearing from God and prophesying, but only a few have the *gift* of prophecy. Here is the way I define the gift of prophecy:

"The gift of prophecy is the special ability that God gives to certain members of the body of Christ to receive and communicate an immediate message of God to his people through a divinely-anointed utterance."[3]

2. *New Apostolic Reformation churches also accept the office of prophet.*

Certain spiritual gifts, but not all, lend themselves to moving the gifted person into an office. When an individual has an office, it simply means that a certain segment of the church has recognized the spiritual gift and that it has publicly authorized the person to use that gift for the benefit of the body. Paul lists several of the offices when he writes, "And He Himself gave some to be apostles, some prophets, some evangelists, and some pastors and teachers" (Eph. 4:11). We have been used to the offices of pastor, teacher, and evangelist. New apostolic churches are now becoming more comfortable with the office of prophet.

To be specific, some of those with whom I associate closely who have been operating in the recognized office of prophet would include Prophet Chuck Pierce, Prophet Paul Cain, Prophet Cindy Jacobs, and others.

It is good that this power principle is being recognized because they are part of the foundation of the church. The Bible says, "[The household of God is] built upon the foundation of the apostles and prophets, Jesus Christ Himself being the chief cornerstone" (Eph. 2:20). Now that this is taking place, God has begun to do things through His church that surpass anything we have seen in history.

3. New Apostolic Reformation church leaders listen care- fully to authentic prophecies.

The reason that God has provided prophets is so that His will can be heard, understood, and obeyed. The major source of the revelation of God is the Bible, and no authentic prophecy could ever contradict the Scriptures. But there are many things that God wants to tell us today that cannot be found in the Bible. Biblical revelation is known by the Greek word *logos,* while contemporary revelation through prophecy is known as *rhema.* Because they are both the word of God, we must not neglect either one.

I use the adjective "authentic" to modify prophecy because, unfortunately, there are many spurious prophecies going around. In fact, because of some bad experiences with unau- thentic prophecy, some have gone overboard and rejected the ministry of prophecy in general. They shouldn't do this any more than they should reject pastoral ministry because of some bad pastors or teaching ministry because of some bad teachers, both of which are common enough. Seemingly in antici-pation of this, Paul writes, "Do not quench the Spirit. *Do not despise prophecies.* Test all things; hold fast what is good" (1 Thes. 5:19-21, italics added). In other words, one of the ways of quenching the Spirit is to reject prophecy, and we don't want to do that.

How Does This Work?

I will conclude this chapter with an illustration of one of my closest friends who has both the gift and the recognized office of prophet, Bill Hamon. He is the author of *Prophets and Personal Prophecy* (Destiny Image), the book that helped me the most during my paradigm shift toward understanding prophecy.

First, this is Bill Hamon's personal testimony: "I have been moving in prophetic ministries since I was eighteen years old. I'll be sixty-two this summer, so it's been a few years. I can say, both honestly and conservatively, that over the last forty years I have laid hands on and prophesied over 30,000 individuals from all parts of the world. Many have also proph-esied over me. At times I have prophesied for six, seven, or eight hours over two or three hundred people in one sitting. The anointing just seems to get going better and stronger the further I go."[4]

Hamon spoke these words on a panel in a national meet-ing in 1996. Pastor Gary Greenwald, who was moderating the panel, introduced him as follows: "Not long ago, I asked Dr. Bill Hamon to come to our church and to prophesy over the people. After he prophesied over three of my pastors, I decided to test him. I put a car salesman in the seat, and I said, 'This is another one of my pastors.' When Dr. Hamon laid hands on him, he prayed a bit in tongues, stopped and said, 'Huh?' Then he prayed in tongues a little more, stopped and said, 'Huh?' He said, 'I don't know what kind of a pastor you are—all I can see are spark plugs, pistons, and a car that won't go!'"

Gary Greenwald said, "The fear of the Lord came on me. I decided never to try to fool God's prophets again!"[5]

Notes

1. John MacArthur, *Charismatic Chaos,* (Grand Rapids MI: Zondervan Publishing House, 1992), p. 51.
2. Jack Deere, *Surprised by the Power of the Spirit* (Grand Rapids MI: Zondervan Publishing House, 1993), p.. 212.
3. C. Peter Wagner, *Your Spiritual Gifts Can Help Your Church Grow* (Ventura CA: Regal Books, 1979, 1994), p. 253.
4. Bill Hamon in an unpublished address given at the National Symposium on the Postdenominational Church held at Fuller Seminary, Pasadena, California, May 20-23, 1996.
5. Gary Greenwald at the above mentioned national symposium.

PRINCIPLE FOUR:

MIRACULOUS HEALING

When you fly to Maui, Hawaii, and approach the Kahalui airport, the most prominent landmark down below will be the huge structure of the First Assembly of God. What's more, if you are sick, you can go into that building during any of their weekend or midweek services and know ahead of time that you can receive personalized healing prayer.

Where Healing the Sick Is Routine

Pastor Jim Marocco is a long-time friend. I love the way that he forthrightly and unpretentiously obeys the Scripture: "These signs will follow those who believe: In My name . . . they will lay hands on the sick, and they will recover" (Mark 16:17-18). Healing the sick, in his church, is not something that is done from time to time, nor is it a low-key invitation to those who might choose to stay late after the service. It is just as much a part of what the church usually does at its regular meetings as is worship, prayer, welcoming visitors, the sermon, the announcements, or taking an offering.

During the worship time, after singing a few songs, Pastor Marocco simply invites all those who need prayer for healing to come forward. Since all are standing anyway, it is not at all disruptive for twenty or thirty or more to slip out of their seats and to come up front. The entire pastoral staff is waiting there with small bottles of oil in their hands. While the band plays softly in the background, every person who comes forward is anointed with oil and prayed for according to their need. When that is over, the congregation resumes singing worship songs and the meeting goes on.

Normally any number of reports will come in during the following week of substantial, verifiable healings that have occurred as a direct effect of the healing prayer in the services. In other words, miraculous healing is a regular part of the ministry of First Assembly, and everybody in town, believers and unbelievers, knows it. Little wonder that the church has been growing steadily for years.

Are "Faith Healers" on the Lunatic Fringe?

Praying for miraculous healing in church services is something that I did not learn in seminary. In fact I can recall that some of my professors would make reference to "faith healers" as if they should be included in the lunatic fringe. Somehow the idea was planted in my mind that the reason we read in the Bible about Jesus and the apostles healing the sick was that medical science had not yet developed in those pre-scientific days, so miracles were more useful then than they would be now. Now that we have doctors and hospitals and health insurance and pharmacies, we have a much better way.

In fact, most of the theologians who taught me had been influenced, directly or indirectly, by renowned Princeton theologian Benjamin Warfield, whom I have referenced earlier. He, we may recall, was an influential proponent of cessationism. Here are Warfield's observations about the biblical accounts of miraculous healings:

> My conclusion then is, that the power of working miracles was not extended beyond the disciples upon whom the Apostles conferred it by the imposition of their hands. As the number of these disciples gradually diminished, the instances of the exercise of miraculous powers became continually less frequent, and ceased entirely at the death of the last individual on whom the hands of the Apostles had been laid.[1]

Most people these days who read this quote from Warfield will be totally amazed that such things were actually being taught in our finest seminaries a generation or two ago. It is so far from the thinking and experience of today's cutting-edge pastors and other Christian leaders that it seems unbelievable. But it was certainly influential back then. During the first twenty years of my ministry I myself honestly believed that Warfield's position was true.

Preaching *Against* Miraculous Healing

Doris and I spent our first 16 years of ministry as field missionaries in Bolivia. I was strongly anti-Pentecostal at the time. I preached against the idea that God does miraculous healings today. I couldn't have tolerated Jim Marocco's healing services. When faith healer Raimundo Jiménez came to our city from Puerto Rico, I strongly admonished my church members not to attend his open-air meetings where miracles were supposed to happen. My first disappointment came when I found that they attended anyway, and then I became extremely perplexed when some of them even testified to being healed! However, I was able to rationalize it all away as some sort of clever fake because that is what I had learned to do in seminary.

Now, of course, my whole way of theologizing and interpreting the Bible and practicing ministry, and teaching my students has turned around 180°. I tell this story because to a large degree my personal paradigm shift is the story of the Christian church in general over the last two or three decades. Granted, there are still a few pockets of cessationism here and there, mostly in the Western world. But, generally speaking, most churches in most countries of the world pray for the sick and see miraculous healings on a regular basis. Many people choose to follow Christ because they have discovered that He cares for their bodies as well as for their souls.

Evangelism with Miraculous Healing

We now live in the period of the greatest spiritual harvest that the world has ever known. The widespread ministry of miraculous healing found in churches all over the globe has been one of the causes, not an effect, of this unprecedented wave of evangelism and church growth. When Jesus ministered, He healed the sick as routinely and as predictably as does Jim Marocco. When Jesus sent out His disciples to preach the kingdom of God, part of their message was literally to demonstrate tangibly that God has power to heal the sick.

The Bible says that healing miracles actually *validated* the ministry of Jesus. Some might think that the ministry of the Son of God would need no physical validation, but apparently it did. When Peter preached his famous sermon on the day of Pentecost, he told the crowd that Jesus of Nazareth

---

Miracles pave the road to effective and fruitful evangelism

---

was "a man attested to God to you by miracles and wonders and signs which God did through Him in your midst" (Acts 2:22). We can conclude that Jesus' ministry was more powerful *with* miraculous healing than it would have been *without* it. And that is the reason that He equipped and sent out His apostles to do the same.

John, of course, was one of those apostles. Years later, when he wrote the Gospel of John, he organized the whole book around seven of Jesus' miracles: changing water to wine, healing a young boy, healing a cripple, feeding 5,000, walking on water, healing a blind man, and raising a dead man. He also said that "Jesus did many other signs" (John 20:30). Why did Jesus do so many signs and wonders? According to John, there was one central reason: "[these signs] are written that you may believe that Jesus is the Christ, the Son of God, and that believing you may have life in His name" (John 20:31). In other words, miracles pave the road to effective and fruitful evangelism.

Signs and Wonders in China

To bring it up to date, the greatest evangelistic harvest in history is now taking place in China. It is reported that some 20,000 to 35,000 persons *per day* are being born again there. No one knows exactly, but some estimate the total number of Christians in China as 100 million, and I have even heard 140 million.

What role do signs and wonders play in this remarkable harvest? It is just as John said it should be. One of the top experts on China, Carl Lawrence, reports: "The single spark that started this prairie fire [in China] were signs, wonders and miracles. A report from the conservative Lutheran China Study Center in Tao Fung Shan, Hong Kong, concludes that 80 to 90 percent of Christians in rural China are the result of a miracle of healing, casting out of evil spirits, or divine intervention, and of first-hand witness' testimonies."[2]

Greater Works?

Apostolic churches, by and large, take a literal interpretation of John 14:12: "Most assuredly, I say to you, he who believes in Me, the works that I do he shall do also; and greater works than these will he do because I go to my Father."

For example, Gary Greenwald, whom I mentioned in the last chapter, tells this remarkable story: "There was a boy by the name of Bree Farrow in one of my meetings. He was so skinny. He was yellow and jaundiced, and they told me that his liver was dead. He was twelfth on the national list to get a liver transplant, but they didn't think he would live until one was available. I prayed for him, and God's anointing came on me. The boy fell down crying. I walked out because I had to get to my next meeting.

"His aunt later came to me and said, 'Bree went out jogging and skate boarding the morning after you prayed for him. He had so much energy! When he got back, he rode his bike all the way down to the beach. His color is all back. When the doctors took the tests, they said that his liver had regenerated. There was a brand new liver, and he has been released.' He is totally healthy today, and God gave him a new liver by His miraculous power."[3]

Gary Greenwald told this story to around 500 or 600 apostolic leaders attending the National Symposium on the Postdenominational Church in 1996. I was very interested to note that the audience reacted with applause, but without surprise. Virtually all of those leaders had seen miracles like this from time to time. Many could tell similar stories.

Healing Teeth

Not everyone agrees how "greater works" than Jesus did should be defined. Certainly raising the dead would be hard to top. Hardly anyone would say that there is anything greater than regenerating lost sinners and making them new creatures. Nevertheless, for several years dental miracles have seemed to attract a good bit of attention. I first met people whose teeth had been supernaturally filled in Argentina in the 1970s when traveling with Omar Cabrera. Since then, it has become virtually commonplace in Argentine churches across the theological spectrum. In the 1990s the phenomenon spread to Brazil where, unlike Argentina, the preponderance of fillings and crowns were genuine gold!

I would not doubt that some readers could begin to question my authenticity because of statements like this. But I would assure them that I personally have visited Argentina and Brazil enough times over the past few years to be able to stake my reputation on affirming that dental miracles have truly been happening. A false report here and there, disproved by a dentist, is regrettable, but it must be seen as the exception, not the rule.

I mention this because, for many, it is more difficult to believe in reports of divine healing of teeth than reports of divine healing of cancer, especially if an ordinary silver filling is changed to gold which has happened frequently. I have a statement from a professional metallurgist, who is a Christian believer, stating: "Don't underestimate this sign; if it can be verified, then it is more spectacular to the scientific community than a virgin birth, medical healing, or even the parting of the Red Sea."

A Challenge to Science?

Why is this? It is because scientists are unanimous in agreeing that only a nuclear reaction can change metallic substances, and this is always in the direction from a more expensive metal to a cheaper one. This metallurgist says, "If it can be verified that mercury amalgam fillings have changed to gold, then this is a sign that God has taken off the gloves with regard to the world of science, and the world's preoccupation with it as the source of truth."

When I first read this, it occurred to me that this might well be what God has in mind. The Bible says that "God has chosen the foolish things of the world to put to shame the wise" (1 Cor. 1:27).

We live in a day when miraculous healing is making a comeback. Seeing God's power manifested in physical healings is just as important today as it was in Jesus' time. It is common in other parts of the world, but I believe that churches like Jim Marocco's church on Maui will also be multiplying here in America.

Notes

1. Benjamin Breckenridge Warfield, *Miracles Yesterday and Today: Real and Counterfeit* (Grand Rapids MI: William B. Eerdmans Publishing Company, 1918, 1965), pp. 23-24.
2. Carl Lawrence, *The Coming Influence of China* (Gresham OR: Vision House, 1996), p. 67.
3. Gary Greenwald in an unpublished address given at the National Symposium on the Postdenominational Church, Pasadena, California, May 20-23, 1996.

PRINCIPLE FIVE:

DEMONIC
DELIVERANCE

In the mind of Jesus the normal thing was for His follow-ers to go out and to spread the message of the kingdom of God by, among other things, casting out demons.

He sent out the twelve apostles with "power over un-clean spirits to cast them out" (Matt. 10:1). He later sent out seventy disciples and they returned saying, "Lord, even the demons are subject to us in your name" (Luke 10:17). Then He said, "These signs will follow those who believe: In My name they will cast out demons" (Mark 16:17).

Evangelism with No Deliverance?

Why isn't this normal anymore? It is not unusual these days to observe a massive evangelistic event involving the ex-penditure of millions of dollars and attracting tens of thousands of attendees come and go with no reports of a single demon being cast out. Many leaders whom I know would affirm that this is bona fide "biblical" evangelism, but I sincerely doubt if Jesus would be in agreement.

A major reason for this is that a preponderance of today's Christian leaders were not taught in seminary that casting out demons could be a vital part of effective evangelism. In seminary, I was taught to believe in the devil—our spiritual enemy No. 1. I was also taught that the devil worked through the world and the flesh, so we had to keep our guard up. But demons? No one taught me how demons behave and what they do. I knew that in theory our enemy attacked through the world, the flesh and the devil, but I didn't get much information about the third part—the devil—and his modus operandi. I went out from seminary to serve the Lord for 16 years as a missionary in Bolivia, and I didn't see a single demon all that time!

Since then I have come to realize that it is extremely important to know about and to know how to deal with the demons of various kinds that the devil employs to do his dirty work of stealing, killing, and destroying. This is a power principle that I believe we need to elevate, once again, to a primary position in evangelistic outreach. Jesus would consider it normal. We should do the same!

In Colombia, Deliverance Counts!

To understand how powerful demonic deliverance can be today, let's go to Bogotá, Colombia. César Castellanos pastors what may be the fastest growing megachurch in the world outside of Nigeria—The International Charismatic Mission. The church has outgrown its facility and it is leasing an indoor basketball stadium that seats 18,000 for its multiple services. At this writing they count around 50,000 *cell groups* in the church. How did this church grow to such gigantic proportions?

There are, of course, many factors which enter into the answer to that question. A principal one, however, is the systematic practice of demonic deliverance. Hundreds of unbelievers get saved through the ministry of The International Charismatic Mission every week. Because of the dismal spiritual atmosphere in Colombia with widespread witchcraft and many other forms of the occult, combined with rampant idolatry in the Catholic Church, an extremely large percentage of new converts are severely demonized. While it is true that the experience of being born again evicts many demons, it is equally true that in some cases they do not all leave. The new believers need help. My friend, Harold Caballeros, says, "As any fisherman can tell you, when we catch a fish we need to clean it right away!"

Cleaning the Fish

César Castellanos makes sure that his fish are cleaned. As part of the package of accepting Christ and joining the church, every new convert is required to go away for a three-day spiritual retreat. One of the purposes of the retreat is to see that each convert receives the ministry of deliverance. The skilled deliverance teams make sure that any demons that did not go at their conversion experience are summarily cast out. Casting out demons in Bogotá is just as normal as Jesus thought it should be!

It is fairly easy to come up with examples like this from the Third World, but not in the Western world. We could show how deliverance plays a key role in the amazing Argentine revival which has been sustained for 17 years. Casting out demons triggered the 25-year process of transforming Almolonga, Guatemala, the only city so far that

---

*Most churches in Nepal
are started with congregations
made up entirely of persons
who have been delivered from demons.*

---

could clearly be considered transformed, in the past tense. Most churches in Nepal are started with congregations made up entirely of persons who have been delivered from demons. These are just examples that could be multiplied indefinitely. But here in the United States we have few such examples.

Let's Get With It in America!

In my opinion, this needs to change if we ever expect to see the true outpouring of the Holy Spirit that we have been praying for. My observation is that the ministry of demonic deliverance is at a very low level in American churches across the board. No city that I know of in America offers the services of casting out demons to its citizens. If the average person wanted to be delivered from demons, they would have no idea of where to go for help. Unless we improve on both of the above, we can have little expectation that out cities will be transformed. We can keep praying for this, but we will see few answers if we don't begin to systematize demonic deliverance.

Can this happen? It all depends.

For one thing, the body of Christ is now in a better position for this than we have been in generations. Historically we have had our ups and our downs. At the beginning of the last century Pentecostals began to cast out demons, but they were severely criticized by "respectable" Christians. Pentecostals then decided to become more "respectable" after World War II, so many of them no longer emphasized demonic deliverance as they had in the past. Then the Charismatic Movement came along and it helped us to believe in demons, but it never mobilized us for action on deliverance on a large scale. We were basically stalled out!

Things Are Improving

However, things are improving. For example, Frank Hammond's book, *Pigs in the Parlor* came out in 1973. My friends then classified it as "ridiculous fantasy." However, my friends now classify it as "groundbreaking!" What a change!

Belief in demons has begun to mainstream. Respected professors such as Charles Kraft, Neil Anderson, Tim Warner, and Fred Dickason have helped greatly. Dynamic pastors such as John Wimber and Jack Hayford have moved us along. Seasoned missionaries who saw it on the field became bold enough to begin to share their experience with more traditional American congregations. As a result, growing numbers of American pastors now have a paradigm for biblical demonology which they might not have had ten years ago.

But even though an unprecedented number of American pastors now believe in demons, relatively few preach on it. Even fewer have installed a visible, local church deliverance ministry. Why? Well, while some believe in demons they really don't think they are much of a threat to their congregations. Then there are others who have chosen to avoid such "spooky" things for fear of alienating some of their church members. As an excuse, some will say, "I believe in demons, but my congregation isn't ready."

What Have We Learned?

Generally speaking, Christian leaders are now over the most formidable barrier to deliverance ministries. They now at least believe in the seven premises of basic demonology. In fact, some seminaries are now teaching them. Here are the seven:

1. There are such things as demons.
2. Demons are beings with distinct personalities.
3. Demons are active throughout the entire human population.
4. The intent of demons is evil—to cause as much misery as possible in this life and in the life to come.
5. Demons are organized under a hierarchy of leaders with Satan at the head.
6. Demons have considerable superhuman power through which they execute their wicked desires.
7. Demons have been defeated by Jesus' blood and they are therefore vulnerable to direct confrontations empowered by the Holy Spirit working through believers.

We Need to Move Up a Level

While we may have come a long way, we are not yet at the

level of demonic deliverance needed to sustain a process of revival or city transformation in our nation. We need to move from "Demonology 101" to "Advanced Demonology", so to speak. And the sooner we do it the better!

Among some of those who do have a basic paradigm characterized by the seven premises above, there linger two widespread notions about demons and deliverance which, in my opinion, are much more than benign differences of opinion. They are actually *barriers* to allowing more people to experience true freedom in Christ. They, unfortunately, contribute significantly to quenching the work of the Holy Spirit in our day.

What are these two harmful notions?

Christians Cannot Be Demonized

A major stumbling block to moving to a new level of demonic deliverance in America is the notion that Christians are immune to the type of demonic activity which calls for personal deliverance. Unfortunately, this is the official position of such a prestigious denomination as the U.S. Assemblies of God. One of their theological professors says, "We do not believe for a moment that a believer can be demonized. But we do believe that a believer can become an unbeliever! We do believe that a man of faith can renounce that faith! When this happens, the possibility of demon possession is very real, for unbelievers can be demonized!"[1]

This respected teacher holds strong opinions about deliverance ministries in our churches. He goes on to say, "It is unscriptural to lay hands on believers to cast out demons. Sincere but misguided people seek to do it, but they are wrong—very wrong!"[2]

Not all Pentecostals agree. Jack Hayford, for example, says, "Demons do trouble and torment believers, and sometimes oppress them with burdensome bondage. Clearly, it would be improper to describe this oppression as 'possession,' but with equal certainty it would be foolish to deny the reality of the bondage. It would be worse to refuse or be unwilling to become equipped to minister to such soul-level affliction."[3] I agree with Jack Hayford.

Why This Is a Serious Barrier

Why would the doctrine that Christians can't be demonized be such a barrier? First, it leaves us impotent to free many Christians from bondage and misery. My wife, Doris, has sustained a powerful ministry of personal deliverance for years. Her book, *How to Cast Out Demons* (Renew), is being used in many churches as a fundamental guidebook for deliverance ministries. I can't count, by way of example, how many Christian pastors have been delivered from addictions to pornography through her ministry. Why should they remain in bondage? In fact, Doris will minister deliverance only to believers. She could cast demons out of unbelievers, but unless unbelievers are willing to be saved, the demons will return, often bringing more with them.

Furthermore, if Christians are immune to demonic invasion, as some would contend, deliverance will naturally take a back seat for training leaders in seminaries and Bible schools. Such teaching will also prevent local churches from developing effective deliverance ministries. Worse yet, it actually forces some believers to seek help elsewhere. In Mexico, for example, it is reported that alarming numbers of Pentecostal believers routinely seek help from witches in times of personal crisis.

Is My Way the Only Way?

The second barrier to seeing deliverance moving to new levels in America is the notion, common among deliverance ministers, that their way of doing deliverance is superior to all others. As an outsider I am a bit mystified by this attitude. I know many deliverance ministers who have different methods, but the bottom line with all of them is that demons are evicted.

It seems logical to me that God would assign different ministries and activities to those who have the gift of deliverance. At least that is what 1 Corinthians 12:4-6 sets forth as the rule. This is necessary because demons are different and strongholds in individuals inviting demonic activity are also different. Some demons leave at conversion, some leave at baptism, some can be self-delivered, some leave at a church altar call, some leave through a truth encounter, and some require a major league power encounter before they will go. The body of Christ needs different deliverance ministers who are equipped to handle deliverance at different levels and in different situations. I would say, the more variety of deliverance ministries the better!

What I would also like to see is a networking of deliverance ministers and ministries so that referrals begin to take place. The medical profession does it. An orthopedic surgeon would not attempt a heart transplant. The patient would be referred to a heart surgeon. The legal profession does it. An estate planning attorney would not defend a client suspected of murder. The client would be referred. But apparently we are not yet ready for this in the ministry of deliverance.

Retooling for Revival

Deliverance ministry is foundational for revival. I would urge the American church to place demonic deliverance higher on their priority list than it has been. Here are four things that would make a huge difference in our cities and in our nation if we Christian leaders would determine to implement them:

1. Local churches should become the principal base for deliverance ministries across the country. Parachurch agencies should continue to do whatever they can, but they cannot substitute for local churches.

2. At least ten percent of the life-giving churches in a given city should have highly-visible, efficiently-functioning deliverance ministries. I don't believe that every church could or would want to do this. But with ten percent of the churches focused on structured, proactive, accessible deliverance ministries that maintained the highest levels of integrity and accountability, we would be tooled for city transformation.

3. We should use fewer euphemisms and more biblical language. The Bible repeatedly refers to this ministry as "casting out demons," and we will have greater success if we do the same. Contemporary terms such as "prayer counseling," or "spiritual ministry," or "freedom in Christ," or "spiritual liberation," or "breaking bondages," have a degree of validity but, all in all, a much lower level of impact than the biblical term.

4. We must enlarge our army of deliverance ministers. Not

only should numbers of deliverance ministers be multiplied, but I think we should go on to develop broadly accepted certification for them, such as we have for C.P.A.s or pharmacists or even haircutters. It would also help if we could devise ways and means of compensating fulltime or part-time deliverance ministers.

Positioned for Revival

I believe that we are now positioned for revival. We are at a place where we can boost deliverance ministries to unprecedented levels. If we decide to do it, I promise you that we will have God's help. After all, why did Jesus come? "For this purpose the Son of God was manifested, that He might destroy the works of the devil" (1 John 3:8). This is the river of God. He wants us to move with Him in destroying the works of the devil so that we can receive that great outpouring of the Holy Spirit on our land that God desires we should have!

Notes
1. Morris Williams, "Do Demons Have Power to Invade Believers?" *Power Encounter: A Pentecostal Perspective* (Springfield MO: Central Bible College Press, 1989), p. 184.
2. Ibid., p. 182.
3. Jack Hayford, "Demons, Deliverance, Discernment," *Ministries Today,* July-August 1999, pp. 22-23.

PRINCIPLE SIX:

POWERFUL
PRAYER

In his book, *The House of the Lord*, Francis Frangipane teaches that the power of God for city transformation will be released as the pastors of a city perceive their churches to be congregations of one citywide church and as they begin to pray fervently together. He experimented with this in his home city, Cedar Rapids, Iowa. While he was doing it, the state of Iowa was suffering from an 11 percent increase in violent crime. However, at the same time the city of Cedar Rapids enjoyed a 17 percent *decrease* in violent crime. The FBI then classified Cedar Rapids as the safest city of more than 100,000 people in the United States for its statistical year.[1]

This is just one example of *powerful* prayer. I emphasize the word "powerful" because not everyone has recognized the difference between powerful and mediocre prayer. Some, in fact, assume that because all prayer is presumably good, then all sincere prayers are equal in the eyes of God. To them, categorizing certain prayers as wimpy and other prayers as awesome would be wrong.

Everyone Knows How To Pray

What was I taught about prayer in seminary? Frankly, I can't remember much about it. I know that the seminary didn't offer courses in prayer while I was there. I was instructed in how to preach and baptize and serve communion, but I can recall no lessons in how to pray or even in how to lead a prayer meeting. There was an assumption that prayer was important, but it was also assumed that everyone knew how to pray well enough. Learning how to pray would somehow take care of itself.

I am just guessing, but one reason why prayer did not have a higher place in the seminary curriculum might have been that my professors, by and large, were Calvinists. Calvinism takes a very high view of the sovereignty of God, stressing

---

The sovereign God apparently has chosen to order His creation in such a way that many of His actions are contingent on the prayers of His people.

---

predestination. They would have a hard time with the title of Brother Andrews' book, *And God Changed His Mind* (Chosen Books), even though we read accounts in the Bible of God doing that very thing. I remember hearing comments from some professors that prayer will change *you*, but it is not intended to change the course of events that God has already predetermined.

For a good many years after seminary, that was essentially my view of prayer. Consequently, even though I always went through the routine of prayer, I could report very few examples of dramatic answers to prayer. Looking back I would say that, yes, I prayed, but it was not *powerful* prayer.

Effective and Fervent Prayer

I now take a more literal interpretation of James 5:16, "The effective, fervent prayer of a righteous man avails much." *Effective* and *fervent* prayer is not the same as prayer in general.

One of the things that helped me understand the dynamics of prayer was coming across a chapter title in Jack Hayford's book, *Prayer Is Invading the Impossible* (Ballentine Books): "If We Don't, He Won't." Notice that Jack Hayford did not say, "If we don't, He *can't*," because obviously God can do anything that He wants to do. But Hayford, in my opinion, has a much more satisfactory view of the outworking of God's sovereignty than we tend to learn from Calvinism.

Here's how I think about it. True, God is sovereign and He can do anything He wants to do. The sovereign God, however, apparently has chosen to order His creation in such a way that many of His actions are contingent on the prayers of His people. It is as if God has a Plan A that He will implement if believers pray fervently and effectively. If they do not, He then has a Plan B. God's Plan A is obviously better for all concerned than Plan B. However, the choice, according to the design of our sovereign God, is ours, pure and simple.

Here is the way Richard Foster states it: "We are working with God to determine the future. Certain things will happen in history if we pray rightly."[2] This is extremely important for apostolic-type praying.

Apostolic Praying

Since I have spent many years as a member of traditional churches and many years as a member of new apostolic churches, it is fairly easy for me to highlight the differences. Here are some:

♦ In traditional churches prayer is *incidental* while in apostolic churches it is *central.* Some take prayer so seriously that they have added a pastor of prayer to the church staff.

♦ In traditional churches prayer is *routine* while in apostolic churches it is *spontaneous.* True, there are times in virtually all services where prayer is routinely expected, but in apostolic churches we also hear "Let's stop and pray," followed by unprogrammed prayer action more frequently than in traditional churches.

♦ In traditional churches prayer is *occasional* while in apostolic churches it is *frequent.* During worship, for example, the worship leader may break out in leading the congregation in prayer several times in one service.

♦ In traditional churches prayer is *passive* while in apostolic churches it is *aggressive.* Answers to prayer are expected, they are not surprises.

♦ In traditional churches prayer is *quiet,* while in apostolic churches it is *loud.* During prayer there is much more vocal audience participation and the noise level is notable.

At times the entire congregation will engage in "concert prayer" when everyone is praying out loud at the same time.

♦ In traditional churches prayer is *reverent* while in apostolic churches it is *expressive*. People pray with their eyes open at times, they kneel, they fall on the floor, they lift their arms up and down, and they walk around.

♦ In traditional churches prayer is *cerebral* while in apostolic churches it is *emotional*. There is much more passion in apostolic praying. Some churches keep boxes of Kleenex under the seats because it is expected that certain ones will start weeping during prayer. After a prayer time, many will release their emotion by applauding or even shouting.

Cutting-Edge Prayer in Your Church

It is true that not every new apostolic church would rate a "10" in their prayer life. Most of them, however, are moving up the scale and some quite rapidly. As I have visited apostolic churches across the country, I have observed five very innovative prayer characteristics that, in my opinion, should be widely imitated. These churches are setting the pace for raising the level of powerful prayer in our country. I hope that you begin to do these things in your church if you are not already doing them

1. *Recognizing the office of intercessor.* In the 1970s today's great global prayer movement began. One of the offshoots of that was recognizing the gift and office of intercessor.

We did not hear much about intercessors, per se, in the 1970s, but their profile began to rise in the 1980s, and it was pretty much in place by the 1990s. Most new apostolic churches have organized ministries of intercession. It is not unusual, when I visit a new apostolic church, to be introduced to "Jane Simpson, one of our intercessors," or to "Jack Stevens, he heads up our church prayer ministry." In some churches, special nametags are furnished to intercessors so that some who need prayer can easily find them.

For many years pastors were not aware that certain individuals in their church had been called by God to stand in the gap for the church and its ministry to a much higher degree than was expected of the average Christian. This is partially due to the fact that, as I have explained, all prayer was considered more or less equal. Intercession was not thought of a specific ministry as were evangelism, music, teaching Sunday School, serving as a deacon, or things like that. Fortunately that has changed, and powerful prayer has now been released because intercessors are recognized and even honored for their ministry.

2. *Prayer teams cover all church services.* So many churches now have constant prayer going on during their services that they wonder how they ever functioned without it. Charles Spurgeon was a pioneer of this, referring to a basement room staffed with intercessors under the platform as his "spiritual engine room." Many pastors were aware of what Spurgeon had done, but generating that kind of committed, persistent prayer in traditional churches was not an easy task. One of the reasons was that pastors had little instruction in how to identify and deploy intercessors in their churches.

This has now changed in new apostolic churches. In many of them the intercessors are organized into one or more teams with committed leadership and a strong feeling that the fruit of the ministry of the whole church is dependent to a significant degree on their ministry of lifting up that particular service before God's throne. Often the intercessors pray in a separate room equipped with a monitor on which they can watch the proceedings as they pray.

3. *Pre-service prayer is the norm.* When the intercessors have their own room, the pastors and staff of new apostolic churches make it a habit of spending time in the room with the intercessors before they go out to lead the church services. In some cases the prayer in the room is spontaneous with intercessors walking around the room and praying out loud simultaneously. The staff simply enters the room and joins the group, praying out loud along with the others. Occasionally, one or two intercessors may approach the pastor, lay on hands, and pray for God's special anointing for the service to come.

Other churches are a bit more organized. When the pastor and other platform persons come into the room the intercessors drop everything and gather around the leaders. Sometimes the pastors are kneeling, sometimes sitting, and sometimes standing. Frequently prophecies will come forth as the intercessors seek to hear from God. I know many new apostolic pastors who would no more think of going into the pulpit without that impartation through prayer then they would think of going into the pulpit without a shirt.

4. *Local church prayer rooms.* It is one thing to recognize

intercessors, pray during the services, and pray for pastors before they preach. But many churches are now going further and establishing local church prayer rooms for sustained prayer. These are rooms in churches set aside solely for prayer. They are comfortable, tastefully decorated, pleasant rooms. Many have dedicated telephone and fax lines, and some are equipped with computers connected to the church's web page. Most of their praying is focused on their own congregation and their own community, but increasing numbers are connecting to other prayer rooms in the nation and with prayer networks around the globe through the World Prayer Center.

The ideal of most local church prayer rooms is 24-hour prayer, 7 days a week. It takes a while to attain that, but as a starter they have their prayer rooms up and running for regular hours each day so that church members and others in the community who need prayer know when they can call. Two recent books will be extremely helpful to those who are interested in starting local church prayer rooms: *Making Room to Pray* by Terry Teykl (Prayer Point Press) and *How to Have a Dynamic Church Prayer Ministry* by Jill Griffith (Wagner Publications).

5. *Pastors' Prayer Partners.* I can safely say that more pastors have testified to me that their lives and ministries have been lifted up to a higher level through building teams of personal prayer partners than any other single cause. That is why I have said many times that of all the books I have written, *Prayer Shield* (Regal Books) is the most important one for pastors. Whenever a lay person comes up to me in a conference and asks, "Peter, which of your books would you say I should take home to my pastor as a gift?" I always suggest *Prayer Shield*.

Unfortunately, once intercessors began to be recognized as such, immaturity and lack of experience caused many problems that began to build barriers between some pastors and some intercessors. *Prayer Shield* faces these barriers realistically and helps pastors and intercessors to understand and appreciate each other. Once they get on the same page, unprecedented spiritual power almost inevitably begins to flow into the pastor's life and ministry. The intercessors win, the pastors win, the church wins, and the future becomes brighter.

Other books that I highly recommend for helping pastors to recruit prayer partners is *Preyed On or Prayed For* by Terry Teykl (Prayer Point Press) and *Partners in Prayer* by John Maxwell (Thomas Nelson).

"I Was Going To Kill You!"

I want to conclude this chapter on powerful prayer with an example from the lives of my friends Eddie and Alice Smith, two of the household names in the U.S. prayer movement.

While Alice was shopping in the supermarket, she had a vision waiting in line at the checkout stand. Suddenly she clearly saw someone pointing a gun at her husband in his church office! Like many intercessors would, she reacted immediately. Leaving her basket full of groceries, she rushed out of the store, drove home and closed herself in her prayer closet. Thirty minutes later, she felt a release. She telephoned her husband, and said, "Eddie, are you okay?"

Eddie said, "Yes, I'm okay. He just got saved!"

What happened? A medical doctor who had been battling demons, had loaded his pistol that day and left home to visit Pastor Eddie, whom he did not like. No sooner had he entered the office than he realized that, unexplainably, he had left home so rapidly that his weapon had remained on the kitchen counter. He soon confessed to Eddie, "I was going to kill you and then kill myself!" But, due to Alice's prayer, he ended up a child of God.

Is that powerful prayer, or what?

Notes

1. See Francis Frangipane, *The House of the Lord* (Lake Mary FL: Cre-
    ation House, 1991), pp. 56-57.
2. Richard Foster, *Celebration of Discipline* (San Francisco CA:
    HarperSanFrancisco, 1988), p. 35.

PRINCIPLE SEVEN:

TUNING IN TO
NEW POWER LEVELS

This concluding chapter will be shorter than the others and somewhat different. The first six principles, including the operation of the Holy Spirit, warfare worship, prophecy, miraculous healing, demonic deliverance, and powerful prayer were all emphases that were actually present in some churches while I was being trained in seminary. However, the seminaries I chose were not tuned in to these churches or to these principles. In fact, the more vocal and aggressive leaders of such churches were often dismissed as the "lunatic fringe" by some of my professors. I was taught that respectable Christians did not get involved in such things or associate very much with those who did.

I covered the details of such attitudes in the previous chapters.

New Power Levels

Neither this book on power principles nor any other like it could possibly be a complete book because God's work here on earth is not yet complete. We can write about power principles that we are currently aware of, but it is foolish to think that God has finished revealing all the power principles that He is ever going to reveal.

In my opinion, many Christian leaders are a bit too nostalgic about the first century. This is not surprising because the New Testament was all revealed to us during the first century. Here is where we derive all our basic principles for our Christian lives and ministries. No question about that. However, it is easy to carry that to the extreme that argues that today we need "first century churches." I couldn't disagree more. I think that what we need today are biblical, *twenty-first* century churches if we are going to win our current world to Christ.

Hearing New Things from the Holy Spirit

Nothing in the New Testament says that we should stagnate, live in the past, or be satisfied with the status quo. Jesus' teaching that God provides new wineskins for the new things that He does is very important to understand and to take seriously (see Matt. 9:17). God is decisively pouring out new wine here in the twenty-first century and first-century wineskins were not designed to hold it. This is why the Bible says, "He who has an ear, let him hear what the Spirit says to the churches" (Rev. 2:11).

"Says" is present tense. We certainly should be aware of

what the Spirit has said to the churches through the ages, but even more important for us is to hear what the Spirit is saying today. There is no valid biblical assumption that the Holy Spirit never says anything new. To the contrary, I believe that the Holy Spirit continually says some important things to each new generation that He did not say to previous generations.

Four Newly-Revealed Power Principles

This brings me to the subject of this rather brief concluding chapter. Part of what God expects of us is to tune in to the new things that He is always revealing, in this case the new power principles that He is opening up to us. I want to list four of them in this chapter which I didn't learn about in seminary. But this time, the reason I did not learn them in seminary is because when I went to seminary the Spirit had not yet spoken to the churches about them.

Before I list the four, let me say that these four do not complete the list. They might bring us up to date for now. But God will not be through revealing new things and designing new wineskins until Jesus returns. In the days to come I do not doubt that believers will be using awesome power principles that I could not list today. And this should be expected. Jesus said, "He who believes in Me, the works that I do he will do also; and greater works than these will he do, because I go to My Father" (John 14:12).

While I didn't learn these four power principles when I went to seminary, I did have the privilege of teaching them to my students in Fuller Seminary in the 1990s, and I am currently teaching them to my students at the Wagner Leadership

Institute. I consider them the four most important new concepts related to power ministries that the Holy Spirit revealed
to the churches in the decade of the 1990s. My goal here will
simply be to describe the concepts and to guide you to some
of the up-to-date resources which will give you the details
you need to incorporate them into your ministry for God.

1. Strategic-Level Spiritual Warfare

It was back in the legendary congress on evangelism called
Lausanne II in Manila where the concept that there might be
such things as "territorial spirits" became known to the wider
body of Christ. That was 1989, the threshold year into the
decade of the 1990s. Those of us who believed that this was
something the Spirit was truly saying to the churches organized the Spiritual Warfare Network in 1990 in order to begin
to process and communicate what we were hearing. My as-
signment was to serve as the International Coordinator of the
Spiritual Warfare Network, which I have done ever since.

Not surprisingly, God began to reveal this in a congress
on *evangelism*. Strategic-level spiritual warfare emerges from
Paul's teaching that the reason that more people are not being
saved is that "the god of this age" has blinded their minds (see
2 Cor. 4:4). In order to keep people in darkness, Satan has
deployed a whole hierarchy of demonic principalities and
powers, the highest members of which have been assigned
cities, nations, people groups, religions, neighborhoods, in-
dustries or other social networks that bind human beings together. Our marching orders for opening up these people to
the gospel involve wrestling not "against flesh and blood,"
but "against principalities, against powers, against the rulers

of the darkness of this age" (see Eph. 6:12). We call this "strategic-level spiritual warfare."

Resources on strategic-level spiritual warfare:
    I have two books that will give you my best thinking: *Warfare Prayer* (Regal Books) and *Confronting the Powers* (Regal Books). I also highly recommend *Possessing the Gates of the Enemy* by Cindy Jacobs (Chosen Books) and *The Jericho Hour* by Dick Eastman (Creation House). Wagner Leadership Institute offers a concentration on Spiritual Warfare for those who desire in-depth training and impartation.

2. Spiritual Mapping

George Otis, Jr. is the pioneer in the field of spiritual mapping. Spiritual mapping can be seen as the principal research component of strategic-level spiritual warfare. We know that the weapons of our warfare are not carnal, but spiritual (see 2 Cor. 10:4). Our major spiritual weapon is powerful prayer, and the more targeted our prayers are, the more powerful they can be. Spiritual mapping helps us target our prayers accurately. There is no use spending our time in vague, scattered, shotgun prayers when we can use the same amount of time for accurate rifle-shot prayers against the enemy.
    We need to know as much about our enemy and his tactics as we can. No respectable general goes into battle without the best of intelligence. If we hope to push back territorial spirits so that people under their influence can hear the gospel, it is good to have accurate knowledge as to what we are up against. The Bible says, "Lest Satan should take advantage of us, we are not ignorant of his devices" (2 Cor. 2:11). Just think. . . Suppose we *are* ignorant of Satan's devices?

Well, obviously he will take advantage of us! Too many people are being taken advantage of in our cities today. Spiritual mapping helps to reduce our level of ignorance and therefore our level of vulnerability.

Spiritual mapping is to intercessors what X-rays are to a surgeon. No surgeon would want to cut blindly when X-rays can show him or her exactly where to cut. The same is true for spiritual mapping. It provides incredible new power to intercessors.

Resources on spiritual mapping:

George Otis, Jr., has written several books, but his classic is *Informed Intercession* (Regal Books). If you read only one book on spiritual mapping, this must be it. For years to come, this will be our official textbook on the subject. Another interesting and informative book is one that I have edited, *Breaking Strongholds in Your City* (Regal Books). You will like it because it has several chapters by experts in the field such as Bob Beckett, Harold Caballeros, Cindy Jacobs, Victor Lorenzo, and Kjell Sjoberg, plus George Otis, and myself. Wagner Leadership Institute offers a concentration on Spiritual Mapping which will provide you with the highest-level training available today.

3. Identificational Repentance

The basic methodology of spiritual mapping involves asking three questions:

- ♦ What is wrong with our community?
- ♦ How did it get that way?
- ♦ What can we do about it?

Granted, these are not simple questions to answer, especially the one that asks how our community got that way. But when you apply the principles of spiritual mapping you will find that the invisible world has a great deal of influence on the visible world. Spiritual mapping is seeing things as they really are, not as they appear to be.

Almost invariably you will find that sometime in the near or more distant past, your community, *as a community*, has sinned. Usually not once, but multiple times. These corporate sins leave behind wounds which become openings for high-level demonic forces to invade and influence the whole community. Discovering this helps greatly to know how your community got that way.

What, then, can we do about it? God raised John Dawson up in the 1990s to pioneer the field of identificational repentance. Once the sins of the past have been uncovered, those of us alive today and identified with the community can repent of these sins and the blood of Jesus can remit them. I am not speaking of *individual* sins, but of *corporate* sins. How powerful is this? It can remove strongholds that the enemy has been using to invade our communities (for decades or even centuries) and to do his evil work of stealing, killing, and destroying! It can open doors to receiving God's blessing for city transformation.

Resources on identificational repentance:
   The recognized textbook for identificational repentance is John Dawson's *Healing America's Wounds* (Regal Books). I also highly recommend John Sandford's *Healing the Nations* (Chosen Books), Jim Goll's *Father Forgive Us!* (Destiny Image), and *Sins of the Fathers* by Brian Mills and Roger Mitchell (Sovereign World).

4. Territorial Commitment

New apostolic pastors, more frequently than traditional pastors, tend to sense a lifetime call to their church and to their community. The church they pastor is not seen as a mere stepping stone for moving on to a larger church somewhere. This allows pastors to rise to a level of spiritual authority in their community that they could not otherwise attain. It is called "territorial commitment," and this is now recognized as a crucial power principle for city transformation.

Bob Beckett, pastor of the Dwelling Place Church in Hemet, California, was the human instrument that God used to bring territorial commitment to the attention of the body of Christ in the 1990s. For years after he planted the church, it was a mess. It would hardly grow. He experienced five major church splits. There were no finances even for small projects like remodeling the nursery. The pastors in the city were indifferent toward the ministry of other pastors in the city. Then Bob and his wife, Susan, felt the call of God to commit themselves to spend the rest of their lives in Hemet, no matter what. They bought a cemetery plot, and they displayed the deed to the congregation the next Sunday.

The situation changed immediately! The church began to grow, and they are now getting ready to move into a new, modern worship center. Beckett is honored as a leader, and there have been no more church splits. The pastors in the city love each other and support each other. And the city of Hemet itself has seen tangible signs of transformation. Commitment to a territory definitely can make a difference.

Resources on territorial commitment:

The number one book is *Commitment to Conquer* by Bob

Beckett (Chosen Books). Bob and Hemet, California are fea-
tured in George Otis Jr.'s monumental video, *Transforma-
tions* (Sentinel Group). I also deal with territorial commitment in my book, *Apostles of the City* (Wagner Publications).

Conclusion

What we learned or did not learn in seminary actually matters
very little in comparison to having an ear to hear what the
Spirit is continually saying to the churches right now. My
prayer is that the apostolic power principles that you have
learned about in this book will enable you, your friends, and
your church to move to new levels in doing your part to advance the kingdom of God and to bring glory to Jesus Christ!

SUBJECT INDEX

WAGNER
LEADERSHIP INSTITUTE

Founded by Dr. C. Peter Wagner, Wagner Leadership Institute (WLI) trains and equips men and women for leadership in local churches and other ministries.

This radical new approach to education emphasizes practical ministry experience, anointing, and impartation. Because practical training and impartation are the goals of each course, no grades are given for courses, events, or training experiences taken for credit. Nor are there exams. Rather, field research, apprenticeship, mentoring, and ministry experience are deemed as valuable as library research or classroom attendance. Our goal is to equip leaders with the necessary skills for effective ministry. Entrance requirements are not based on academics, but on age, ministry experience, and maturity.

WLI provides an earned training credential for church and ministry leaders who desire ordination, licensing, or other forms of public recognition by awarding diplomas for Associate of Practical Ministry, Bachelor of Practical Ministry, Master of Practical Ministry, and Doctor of Practical Ministry.

For more information on Wagner Leadership Institute visit our website at:

www.wagnerleadership.org

or call us at:

1-800-683-9630

Apostles of the City

How to Mobilize Territorial Apostles for City Transformation

C. Peter Wagner

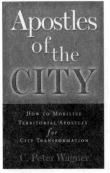

In recent years the Body of Christ has seen some important principles for city transformation set in place. While there have been many short-term successes, city after city reports that their efforts over the long haul are not producing the city transformation that they have worked so hard to accomplish.

So, what are we missing? How can we see our cities become all that God intended them to be? This book examines how recognizing and affirming apostles of the city might well be the most vital missing link for seeing our cities truly transformed!

Discover the answers to many questions, including:

- What strategic changes need to be made in my city in order to see it truly transformed?

- Who is an "apostle of the city," and how are they set in place?

- What are the three crucial concepts I need to know that will lay the proper groundwork for city transformation?

- Is my city prepared for the moving of the Holy Spirit that will bring real transformation in the near future?

This important new book is for everyone who wants to see their city move beyond short-term successes into the genuine transformation that God desires to bring!

Leadership
Paperback • 58p
ISBN 1.58502.006.0 • $6.00

Available at finer bookstores
or by calling toll-free 888-563-5150

Hard-Core Idolatry

Facing the Facts

C. Peter Wagner

This hard-hitting book will help
clear away many questions about
idolatry and how it has perme-
ated churches today. Readers of
this book will:

- Understand the difference
  between hard-core and soft-
  core idolatry

- Feel the pain of God's broken
  heart when His people worship idols

- Recognize idolatry, even in some of our
  churches

- Be able to confront Satan's schemes with more
  understanding and power

- Begin to cleanse their own homes of ungodly
  objects

Christian Living/Spiritual Warfare
Paperback • 43p
ISBN 0.9667481.4.X • $6.00

The Queen's Domain
Advancing God's Kingdom in the 40/70 Window

C. Peter Wagner, Editor

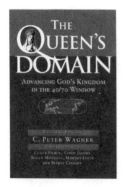

Does prayer really change the world? Without question the answer is yes! This book will encourage any Christian by showing dramatic answers to prayer that has radically changed the world in the 1990s and has put us in the midst of the greatest spiritual harvest the world has ever known. So, where do we go from here?

In *The Queen's Domain*, C. Peter Wagner has pulled together five top Christian leaders and intercessors who show where the Body of Christ is headed in prayer in the new millennium for an even greater harvest! Together they answer many questions including:

- Who is the "Queen" and where is her domain?

- Why are there so many unsaved "Christians" in the 40/70 Window?

- How will fervent prayer for the 40/70 Window have a ripple effect throughout the world?

- How can we transfer wealth from the Queen's Domain into the kingdom of God?

- How is prayer for the 40/70 Window different from prayer for the 10/40 Window?

Spiritual Warfare/Prayer/Missions
Paperback • 127p
ISBN 1.58502.009.5 • $8.00

Available at finer bookstores
or by calling toll-free 888-563-5150

Confronting the Queen of Heaven

C. Peter Wagner

This book takes a look at what is perhaps one of the most powerful spirits in Satan's hierarchy: the Queen of Heaven. Throughout history this high-ranking principality has kept countless multitudes of lost souls blinded to the gospel.

In this book, C. Peter Wagner takes a look at how the Queen of Heaven has accomplished her goals in the past, and how she is manifesting in the world today to keep untold numbers in spiritual darkness. This book will help you discover how God is mounting an assault against this dark force to see the captives set free!

Spiritual Warfare/Missions
Paperback • 42p
ISBN 0.9667481.3.1 • $6.00

Revival!

It Can Transform Your City

C. Peter Wagner

This book takes you beyond city taking to city transformation!

Questions addressed include:

- What exactly is revival?

- Can a city actually be transformed through revival?

- How can Christians move to new levels of spiritual warfare to see revival come?

- What new wineskins is the Holy Spirit using to facilitate revival?

- What steps can be taken to sustain revival in a city?

Discover how the Spirit of God can visibly transform cities through the revival we have been praying for.

Leadership/Spiritual Warfare
Paperback • 63p
ISBN 0.9667481.8.2 • $6.00

Radical Holiness
For Radical Living

C. Peter Wagner

Holiness has long been a topic of great debate. In this easy-to-read book, C. Peter Wagner helps bring clarity to the topic by answering many questions including:

- Can anyone really live a holy life?

- Is there a test of holiness?

- What are the non-negotiable principles for radical holiness?

- How much holiness should be required of a leader?

For any believer who wants to be everything God wants them to be, this book will open the way for them to move to new levels in their Christian lives. Through radical holiness, readers will learn to defeat Satan's schemes and enjoy daily victory in their walk with God!

Christian Living
Paperback • 41p
ISBN 0.9667481.1.5 • $6.00